T0129411

THE ULTIMATE YOU:

How To Be The Best You Can Be In 30 Days or Less...

And Attract Prosperity and Everything of Substance into Your Life

Gilbert Motsaathebe

THE SUCCESS FORMULA

A step-by-step guide for enriching your life, maximising your potential, attaining success, wealth, love and happiness

iUniverse, Inc.
New York Bloomington

iUniverse books may be ordered through booksellers or by contacting:

iUniverse
1663 Liberty Drive
Bloomington, IN 47403
www.iuniverse.com
1-800-Authors (1-800-288-4677)

ISBN: 978-1-4401-9691-1 (sc)
ISBN: 978-1-4401-9692-8 (ebook)

Printed in the United States of America

iUniverse rev. date: 01/13/10

Dedication

For all men, women and children out
there who have always wanted to improve their lives but didn't know how.

The Ultimate You is also a special dedication to
my grandfather April, who will sadly never read it.

He passed away in 2007, while the
book was being composed.

He was the first person to show me the
true application of abundance theory.

I will forever be grateful for his example.

Preface

Congratulations! This could be the most important and smartest investment you have ever made. You are holding in your hands a practical formula that could augment your life with success, money, love and happiness—the success formula that will help you attract abundance in all areas of your life. Imagine the reward of being a fulfilled individual with a positive self and physical image, extraordinary personality and habits, thriving in all areas of your life; and attracting real people of substance and succeeding in happy relationships. This book is based on the concept that the universe is brimming with everything we need to succeed in our lives and that anybody with the right attitude, training and spiritual discipline can attain self-fulfillment. This life-changing concept is derived from abundance theory which sees the universe as generous depending on your attitude, but the heart of this book lies in personal experience. In the following chapters, I will be sharing the secret formula that I learned over the years—which you can emulate in as little time as 30 days to work miracles into your life and influence your destiny.

We often read self-help books that contain novel ideas, but most of the time these books fail because they don't provide us with a tacit roadmap. This book fills that gap by providing tried and tested concrete steps that you can apply.

Each chapter begins with an overview of real issues that may stand between you and the ideal you; then suggests practical steps to deal with them. It ends with a visualisation to enable you to translate what you have just read into action.

There is a power in visualisation. When you go through what you have read or seen you are rehearsing the steps, committing them to memory where they will be available when you need to apply them. Believe me, you will need visualisation for the task that lies ahead as you journey with me to *the ultimate you*. Where appropriate, examples are provided together with sound advice and warnings.

You now have a chance to overhaul your life and improve those areas that you have often neglected simply because you didn't know what to do about them. Consider this book as an awakening call that prompts you to pick up yourself, break the barriers and reach for your full potential faster than you have ever imagined.

As you begin to read the first chapter, remind yourself that you only have 30 days to read and apply everything you learn here. You have a deadline!

If you are a bit nervous, do not fret because I am about to take your hand and walk with you every step of the way.

Yours truly

Gilbert Motsaathebe

Acknowledgement

I want to thank all men and women out there, past and present who have successfully practised the abundance theory knowingly or inadvertently to work miracles in their lives.

I express my gratitude to Dr Dorian Haarhoff who was the first person to read this book when it was still being drafted.

Contents

Chapter 11

"Be the change you want to see in the world." - Mahatma Gandhi

Chapter 1

CHOICE AND CHANGE

How to get on the superhighway to your ideal self

From the moment we are born we are destined to live a fulfilling life full of everlasting joys. Unfortunately most people don't understand this reality. They keep putting up barriers in their minds that prevent them from living a fulfilling life. The true wisdom that is guaranteed to free you from any form of bondage you might find yourself in at the moment starts with a realisation that we have immense power within us to change our situation to whatever we want or desire. As a human being, you are a very fortunate creature. You have been given a gift of life and a universe replete with everything you need. All you have to do is to sow the seed and reap the benefits. It is as simple as this, you have the choice—to succeed or fail.

You are the master of your own destiny and you can make a decision now about what you want in life. This is a generous world. You can choose to become whoever you want to be. However, choice comes with responsibilities. The best of all choices carries more responsibilities, while the poor ones have little or none. The problem is that most people prefer an easy way out and end up settling for less, not being aware of the dent they make in their lives. They inadvertently undermine the power that they possess. Responsibility is a duty. It calls for discipline, dedication and commitment.

Whether you choose a profound life of abundance or the opposite is entirely up to you. A fulfilling life requires sacrifices. You can choose a life of compromise without responsibility and limit your potential or even perish like many others, without having achieved any of your dreams. Or you can refuse to settle for less and choose a fulfilling life today and become your ultimate best.

The journey to a fruitful life full of everlasting joys starts with a choice. You must make a choice to move out of your comfort zone—to leave the shore in order to discover new seas. This is not simple. It could be a matter of frustration, pain and disappointment. We must accept that in today's world with the hectic pace of life and the ups and downs (both interesting and obscure) many people end up living an unhappy and unrewarding life. When this happens these people lose sight of who they really are and often give up on a productive and satisfying life. They feel defeated and forget that they have the potential to change their situation. It need not be like that.

You must refuse to settle for less. You must know that you can always do more. Think about it, what good is life if you are not happy with it? Your situation can be changed 360 degrees. The key lies in mastering the formula that will allow you to change yourself from what you are now to the ultimate best you can be.

YOU and YOU alone are the only one who can change your destiny.

If you want to change something, you must first effect the change within yourself.

When I first started going to the big cities, I was often confronted with people handing me brochures. In these brochures, there would be people promising all kinds of miracles for a fee. I realised that there was a problem. To begin with, if what was being promised here were true, then the very same people handing out these brochures wouldn't be doing that. If those miracles cannot work in their own lives it inevitably means that they are either lying or that there is a problem with their formula.

The thing is if you hope to change something you must change yourself first, otherwise no one will believe you. People need to see that change in you. You must become an embodiment of the change you want. It was none other than the great Mahatma

Gandhi who put it better than anyone else when he said, "Be the change you want to see."

A human being is a unique force of interconnected systems that require mastery and alignment. Being your best self therefore cannot be a smooth-sailing affair. It requires a clear grasp of what I call human management.

Psychologist Sigmund Freud found a human being to be a complex system with energy available to be expended on tasks that are geared for survival. According to Freud, the energy you spend on one task will not be available for another task. That said, you need to nurture and polish all key skills so that they become part of your inborn mechanisms. This will save you energy since the intuitive mechanism will respond effortlessly and fittingly to given situations.

Often people think that to live a virtuous life you need to be lucky or have wealthy family. That's not the case. The journey to self-discovery starts with a simple DECISION, the decision to change. Your life situation will not change until such time that you are sufficiently enraged by mediocrity and decide that you want to do something about it. You need to realise that you can turn your situation around no matter what your current situation is as long as you are in the right frame of mind and know what you are doing. You'll be amazed at how working on one area could lead to abundance and self-fulfilment that you never imagined as the domino effect ripples through all areas of your life.

Make a decision to change and believe in your ability to change.

Napoleon Bonaparte was a firm believer in his own abilities to accomplish anything he set his mind to. During his student days he was always mocked by other students but he made a decision that he would rise to the highest level possible. On his arrival in France, fresh from college, Napoleon told his seniors to throw away books on warfare because he was about to introduce new methods and revolutionise the fighting tactics in spite of his lack of experience. The ripple of his success in artillery was considerable, irrespective of his lack of experience. He was armed only with a conviction to effect the change he wanted, and that's exactly what he achieved. He rose from a mere Army General to become the Emperor of France and dominated European history in a very short space of time.

His secret was an unwavering belief in his ability to make his dream a reality. Hence I advise you to start believing in yourself. Never doubt yourself and never sell yourself short. You can rise above any situation. Eliminating negativities in your system is a big step to success. If you have any negative thoughts erase them immediately and concentrate only on the positive thoughts and those things that you want to attract into your life. Negative thoughts break up your energy cycle and interfere with your natural positive vibration which is critical for a fulfilling life.

You must realise that the true power of effecting a positive change lies in the resultant ripple effect. When you change a small thing other areas will inevitably improve as the change bears fruit. If you still don't have enough motivation to effect change, just think of all the resultant frustrations, emotional drawbacks and complete waste of time if you stay as you are. Think about the reward that you will get when you improve your life. You don't need anything special but a commitment and desire to succeed.

Work hard at changing yourself and the rest will fall into place.

It can take time and effort to perfect your entire life. But if you start at the right point, the time you take can be reduced drastically. You must start with the fundamentals, i.e., You. And you must start now because if you don't you may never start.

This is something that I personally learnt the hardest way. After years of working professionally I ventured into the property industry. I had been told there was money there. For eight good months I didn't make any money in the business. By the end of that year I was so enraged that I immediately wanted to do something about it. I wanted change. That was an eye-opener.

You see, for years I had succeeded in changing jobs with the hope that my life would be perfect. What I didn't know was that I was the problem. I didn't know that I had to change myself. It was only after I realised that I needed to change that my prospects improved. Within a week of having reached a definite decision to change, my attitude improved so drastically that people kept on asking me, "What's happening these days, you are so happy, full of energy." To which I always replied: "I have changed." For the first time, I could feel that everything that I had always wanted was now within reach. That was the beginning of my journey. I challenge you now to stop limiting yourself.

A few years ago I was driving through a beautiful neighbourhood when I spotted a beautiful house which was so magnificent that I immediately fell in love with it.

But there was one problem. It was more than thrice the price I had in mind which was way above what I could afford. I also knew that no bank would be prepared to loan me such a huge amount, but I made a decision that it was the house I wanted. I was honest from the start with the agent. "I am looking for something cheaper but I love this house."

I went straight home and told my sister that I was going to buy that house. How, I didn't know. I remember recalling the expression: where there is a will there is a way. I took the pamphlet with the picture of the house and all the features and the price and studied it so absorbingly that it became vivid in my mind. But the battles still lay ahead. I kept studying the picture until I had no doubt that I would own that house, irrespective of my present situation. Eventually I was so obsessed with the house that I was compelled to come up with ways to make sure that I acquired the money to buy it.

From the above experience I realised that we often undermine ourselves, not knowing how powerful we can be. If only we would challenge ourselves and look deep within we would be able to come up with solutions for any problems we may face. "Our fears are traitors, they make us lose the best we oft might win, by fearing to attempt", wrote Shakespeare in *Measure for Measure.*

I tell you, if you can forget about excuses, challenge yourself and see what happens – at least if you fail you would have tried. It is better to lose a war in the battlefield rather than to lose it in your mind. You must deal with your fear which is basically what stands between us and the best things we want.

My own journey came at a huge price. It took me many years of hard knocks until I found my true self. In my perpetual search for the ideal self, I often had to take unpaid leave to go to work in other parts of the world so that I could learn as much as possible about other people to prepare for the change I needed. The trials, errors and successes prompted me to write this self-help manual. I hope these personal lessons can be of benefit to those who want to reach their peak. Now you can do it without having to put up with all the troubles that some of us experienced.

The power to change or influence your destiny and effect the change you need is all within reach but it solely depends on how far you are prepared to go.

One of the most fundamental and regrettable mistakes we often make is to look down on ourselves not realizing how much we can accomplish, if we simply commit ourselves. We allow outsiders to give us affirmation and inevitably determine how far we can go. When this happens people undermine their true potential and send a message to the brain which in turn builds an imaginary wall to limit true potential. Like a computer, the brain does only what it is told. As the saying goes, "Aim for the moon, because even when you fall you will at least land amongst the stars." A human being is a composite of a super-intensive force – we have so much more power in ourselves than we can ever imagine. All you need is to trust your own power.

Our own beliefs can influence our fate positively or negatively.

What you believe can make you or destroy you. Our beliefs determine our destinies.

Here is an example:

During my research for this self-help book, I came across an article in one of the Oprah Magazines in which well-known talk show host Noeleen Mahol-wana-Sangqu shared her experience on how your own self-belief can change you.

> "I was perceptive as a child, and knew when people were joking and when they were trying to hurt my feelings. While most of the comments were made in jest, one relative often said very negative things about my appearance."

Through her strong self-belief Noeleen never allowed this person to wreck her confidence so when this adult told her, "You are very fat and ugly," Noeleen did not let these destructive words devastate her. This is how she counteracted: "No, that isn't true. I am not ugly and there is nothing wrong with me."

She truly believed that there was nothing wrong with her and refused to affirm what other resentful people were telling her. She substituted the negative thoughts with a positive affirmation and because she chose not to believe people hell-bent on destroying her, her self-confidence remained intact. She succeeded in believing in her own abilities to become what she wanted. "My unwavering self-confidence has made being a television personality a lot easier."

If you can believe in your own abilities, you will be able to stretch yourself to the limit to get what you really deserve. With self-belief there is no stopping you from reaching far beyond the realm of ordinary human beings and achieving even iconic status.

Wherever you are and whatever your situation is, taking certain corrective steps can go a long way towards making you the ultimate best. Self-belief feeds your dreams and helps to make them stay alive. It helps you to stay awake and turn your dream into reality. The mere fact that you acquired this manual means that you are prepared to go to some lengths to bring about the best in you and live your dreams. So I tell you today, go on and make it happen.

The inner working of the mind represents an important cue to your destiny.

The most important pathway in reaching your destiny is to use your mind as an ally. The mind works in amazing ways. Perhaps the most important thing to note is that it operates in terms of images. The secret lies in creating a mental picture. You must use your imagination as a radical point of departure. You can tap into important cues in your mind to influence your destiny through what I call the illustration stage.

Here is how:

1. Find time and sit comfortably on a couch with a notebook and pen. Make sure that you are completely relaxed.

2. Close your eyes briefly to clear your mind of any lingering thoughts.

3. Then still with your eyes closed, think of the kind of person you really want to become. If no image comes to your head, think of any person alive that epitomizes the person you want to become.

4. Make sure that the picture you see is as vivid as possible. Illuminate it as much as you can, put in all the glamour you can think of that really magnifies it. Do not stop until you are a hundred percent satisfied that this is the real picture of the person you want to be.

5. Create a mental picture of that person. Replay it in your mind as if you are watching live footage.

   • Place this person in an ideal place where there is energy, light, glitz and vitality.

   • Have that person dressed in expensive clothes that appeal to you.

   • Give them something to do that really blows your mind, such as signing autobiographies with a multitude of people looking at him or her with admiration and respect.

6. Now turn the picture around and put yourself in that person's place. Imagine you are now switch-

ing off the lights momentarily like they do at the theatre when there is a change of scenes.

7. Then leave everything there and just take this person out naked as he/she is. Leave everything on your couch even the underwear and then jump into the place of the person that you want to be.

8. Then open your eyes and look at yourself.

   • Write down a description of your ideal self – the person you created during your moment of silence.

   • Make photocopies and have one in your bedroom and one next to the bath so that you can look at it constantly to remind yourself of your concept. Place another one next to the mirror so that you can see it when you comb your hair or brush your teeth. Another one in the kitchen and keep one more in your handbag or wallet.

   • Use mnemonic devices to memorise this living picture and refuse to stand for anything that is not congruent with the picture you have of yourself – be it values, behaviour, style, mannerisms, gestures. Anything that you think will not conform to the ideal self.

9. Replay the picture of your ideal self at least four times a day.

   • Each time you go to your place of worship think of your ideal-self so that it becomes the first thing in your mind even when you begin to pray.

- If you are asked to give a word at a ceremony start with this image and you will surely see miracles. Close your eyes briefly and rehash the picture in your head so that when you speak you can see the movie at the same time as you develop the film in your own head.

From now on see yourself in that image and all the steps that you take must conform to that image imprinted in your head. When you walk, emulate the character in your head, which is your ideal self. Leave your real self just there. This is the beginning of the "new you".

As soon as you have mastered this lesson you must make it a habit. Whenever you feel depressed think of it, then play the footage. You will be able to radiate such a great deal of confidence that you never knew existed – and that you never thought you could master. It will be written all over your glowing face and people will begin to notice it.

Key points to remember

Make a decision to change and believe in your own ability to transform your life. Define your own reality and go out there and make it happen.
Don't let negative feelings or comments distract you. Understand that you can have whatever you desire if you set you mind to it by making a firm commitment to yourself. Your efforts must be coordinated and underpinned by a clearly defined vision.

"The dawn has secrets to tell you, don't go back to sleep."
Rumi

Chapter 2

DREAMS

How to Augment Your Abilities to Reach Your Dream

Did you know that many of the most successful people started their journey to success with a dream? Yes they did. It was their implicit confidence in their own abilities to translate their dreams into reality that make them successful. Now, don't you have dreams? I'm sure you do. Everybody does. Don't you have aspirations? Of course you have.

"Dreams are things you contemplate as imaginably possible" – Chambers English Dictionary

Dreams are objects of imagination. There are two types of dreams, namely imagined dreams and sleep dreams. Imagined dreams are those things that you wish to accomplish while sleep dreams are those happenings that you see in your sleep. There is a link between imagined dreams and sleep dreams in that they are both imaginably possible. As human beings we are dreaming creatures, we imagine things both in our sleep and consciously. Most of what we dream about is those things that we strongly desire. Many psychologists such as Freud and Perls believe that dreams are those aspects of our lives that we often take for granted, reject as impossible or suppress in real life. Thus dreams are generally things that dominate or minds. We need to stay awake and make an effort in order to achieve them. Thus sleep dreams can serve as a spring board of action to an imagined dream or ideal achievement. Dreaming of success in your sleep can steer you to phenomenal success that you have always dismissed as impossible. However you must make a concerted effort and sincerely believe in your own ability to achieve what you set out to do. The key to immense success lies in the power of believing in what you can accomplish.

Here are a few examples:

Former South African president Nelson Mandela, who spent 27 of his youthful years in prison, believed that South Africa would one day be free. He refused to give up his dream of a free and united South Africa.

> "I have cherished the ideal of a democratic and free society in which all persons live together in harmony and with equal opportunities. It is an ideal which I hope to live for and to achieve. But if needs be, it is an ideal for which I am prepared to die."

Mr Mandela went on to become South Africa's first democratically elected president in 1994. He preached reconciliation and today the situation in South Africa has stabilised with black and white living in relative harmony—a complete contrast from what it used to be.

Similarly Martin Luther King had a dream.

"I have a dream that one day the sons of former slaves and the sons of former slaves' owners will be able to sit down together at the table of brotherhood." Martin Luther Jr.

Mr King's dream came to fruition and lived on even after his death. Today African Americans whose great-great-grandparents went to America as slaves are now free and live harmoniously with white Americans whose great-great-grandparents enslaved them.

The above examples illustrate the power of sincerely believing in your own ideas. We can achieve anything we can imagine. You must believe the picture you have transfigured in your head and don't stop believing it until you have emulated everything about that image. Get down to work and begin to effect the change now.

Your power lies in the inner working of the mind.

Now, go on dreaming and while at it, make sure you dream big and stay awake to make your dreams a reality. Just believe in them and in your own ability to transform them, and then act to make them come true. It is as simple as this, if you have a dream, you must wake up and work to make it happen. You can never hope to make the dream real in your sleep. This means that your dream must be accompanied by a footprint that channels the actions that will turn it into reality. This manual is about connecting you with positive vibrations of power within you which hold the key to immense success.

I must warn you though. You will have to adapt to a strict regimen which will make you stand out from those who do not know how to be their best. It gives you a competitive edge. When that happens, you will become a role model and everybody will aspire to emulate you; you will be a trendsetter – an embodiment of excellence.

Dreams allow you to take control of your life. They magnify those things that we often take for granted or those that we think are impossible. For this reason it is important to document your night dreams so that you can study them and see if there is anything you can learn from them. They can be the key to unlock your creativity or discover something novel.

Here is how:

1. Keep a very neat notebook next to your bed with a pen tucked in between the pages.

2. Each and every time you wake up from a dream document the entire dream – exactly the way everything happened during the dream.

3. Do not wait till the morning because you are likely to forget the details.

4. When you wake up in the morning study your dream:

   • What did it reveal to you?

   • Is there anything in the dream that speaks to you?

   • If so see if it is achievable and if not ask yourself why it is not achievable or what will it take you to achieve it.

Don't ever underestimate the power of dreams; they may hold the key to your destiny. Don't give up on them. You must also keep a success journal in which you record all your achievements. This will serve as an inspiration.

Key point to remember

Start to pay attention to both your night dreams and imagined dreams or ideals and work at making them come true. You can literally achieve all your dreams if you genuinely believe that you can do so. Believe in your dreams and make them happen!

"Your thoughts have more power than kings to compel you."
T.S. Eliot

Chapter 3

THE MIND

How to Think Big and Positively

The key to any success of any magnitude lies in the mind. Tuning in your mind to what is about to happen ensures that all of your actions and behaviour are in tandem with the picture imprinted in your mind.

Many psychologists believe that we are born with a *tabula rasa* or blank slate. Most of what we do or know are the things that we plant in our minds ourselves.

An example of this is when you constantly tell yourself that you are not good at anything. You tell the mind that you can't do something and as a result it inhibits positive thoughts and limits your actions. Another example is when you continuously tell your children how ugly or useless they are. They will take it as axiomatic that what you are saying is indeed the case and they will continue to have negative feelings about themselves. Sooner or later that will radiate outwards in the form of a negative attitude or energy.

Now, in both these examples, the mind determines the actions or the behavioural patterns that you exhibit in line with the picture that is imprinted on it. It then limits the potential that was possible. You need to start talking positively to yourself and those around you; cultivating only positive and uplifting thoughts that help you develop your potential and elevate you to another level - the highest possible. Make it a habit to think positively and think big. You must aim high, but you must also know exactly what you want so that you do not stray.

The mind is the powerhouse where thoughts are generated and perfected before being put into action

By now you will have perfected your mental picture of who you really want to be (see previous chapter). Now your next move is to activate your mind, thoughts and feelings.

Everything (including all actions that you take and the behaviour you exhibit) is produced and perfected in the mind before it radiates outward. It then follows that you must perfect the game/ battle plan in the mind. You do what your mind tells you. Make it a habit to think positively and eliminate all negative thoughts from your mind. If you think negatively, you will attract negativity into your life; the same thing happens when you think positively all the time. If you see the world as a cruel place with no opportunities for you to reach your dreams, then you are right. It is your reality and that's what you get because all your actions, thinking and feelings will resemble your reality. However, if you think of the world as a generous place filled with everything you need to enrich your life, maximise your potential, attain success in whatever you do, amass wealth, love and happiness, that's what you will get if you align your actions with your reality.

To appreciate what the mind can do, I recommend you get a copy of Napoleon Hill's book *Think and Grow Rich*, in which he talks about the power of thought and desire. You see to be something you are not at present, you first need to believe that you could be it. But how do you do that? You must really want to be different. There must be an urge that will send signals all through your system so that your actions and feelings are all geared towards what you want. If you are ambivalent about the person you want to become, or about exactly what you want in life, then you will have no intrinsic need to change. The same thing applies if you are afraid to take risks in order to grow. You must be prepared to leave your comfort zone - as the saying goes, if you hope to discover the new seas you must be ready to leave the shore.

Aim to be like a shining star

Your mind has a pull and push effect. When you think positively, you are pushing away all the negative thoughts and feelings and pulling in all positive and good things in your life. You will begin to behave in a positive manner and become a blessing to those around you, attract positive people and all that is in line with your frame of mind. This helps us to really enjoy our lives and reach our dreams or ideal selves. You will know that you have truly accomplished the ideal self when you feel like a shining star. At that level you will be the centre of attraction, beauty, love, happiness and appreciation.

When I was in Tokyo several years ago a gallant young man in an immaculate suit and shoes made a grand entrance at an upmarket restaurant where I was having drinks with an acquaintance. He looked great and exhibited a clearly nurtured etiquette and mannerisms, and he exuded a personality aura that was enlivening. I was really impressed. I carried that picture in my mind for a long time and even wanted to emulate his personality and look like him.

I thought about him today as I went about my daily activities, and even now as I write this page that image is still fresh in my mind. He is the man at the back of my mind, and he nudges me all the time to behave in a certain way. So I have a mental image that I use as a model of what I want. This means that I am not ambiguous about what I want. You must have a clear picture of who you want to be—whether you paint it in your head using your own imagination or you adopt a certain person as your role model.

You could do it through imitation of the behaviour. Yet this will be punctuated by your own unique personal traits. No one person is exactly the same. Even if you copy someone there will always be that something unique about you that will make you stand out and set you apart from the person you are modelling on. This will allow you to fashion an engaging frame of mind or attitude that will propel you to the thrilling success you have envisaged.

You will then find it easy to fashion in small changes in the broader framework that will flesh out the entire repertoire of your ideal self. This will propel you in the right direction.

Believing in your own dreams and your ability to translate them into reality is an essential key to self transformation

Your own ideas about yourself and your faith in those ideas, no matter how big or small, determine your destiny. You can have a grand plan for just about anything, but if it isn't amplified by any sincere belief in your own capacity to execute the plan and bring it to fruition by yourself it will be of little or no use at all.

Our personal and professional battles are designed, fought, won or lost in our minds. Motivational speaker Dr Creflo Dollar compares the mind to a battleground because it is the place where ideas, actions and behaviour are perfected long before they physically materialise. This is what is referred to as intra-communication level in communication literature.

It is important to understand that something that is apprehended in the mind is beyond the realm of physical reality and only conscious efforts on our part will help to transform the reflection into its physical equivalent.

Now that you have mapped your goal as instructed in Chapter 1, it is time to have a short-term goal which is part of the long-term one so that you can make sure that each an every step you take brings you closer to your real self i.e. *the ultimate you.*

Conversely, of all the destructive forces on earth that you can think of, the mind is the most destructive. It can either destroy or build. By that I mean the seed is first planted in the mind which waters it until it is fully grown. This means that it is really within you; our thoughts and any limitation we place on them define who we are. Therefore you need to begin by changing your perception of yourself. You can easily achieve this by replacing all the negative thoughts and energy with positive vibrations.

Here is how:

1. Take a blank page and draw a table with two columns.

2. At the top of the first column write negative thoughts or attributes and write positives on the other.

- Next to negative write destructive and next to positive write constructive in brackets. This is where you will start developing a list of those behaviours that you do not want and those that you would like to attract.

3. Write all negative thoughts that flash across your mind, and those positive ones in the appropriate column.

   - Write as much as you can recall and don't censor yourself.

4. Now, try to replace each an every negative thought you have written down with the positive equivalent.

5. Then read this list everyday for ten to twenty minutes and commit all these positive words to memory.

6. Once you have done this, strive to attract anything that will bring about the positive, either by action, speaking or anything you can imagine.

7. Every time negative thoughts flash across your mind or appear in your life, immediately root them out.

   - Constantly eliminate any negative energy in the form of thinking or feeling. Only their positive equivalent will dominate your thoughts and direct your actions.

   - Maintain only positive thoughts.

8. Remember that the mind is like a computer: it does what you tell it to do. If you honestly think of yourself as a happy person, the mind takes that in and it will endorse that image.

• 18th century novelist Daniel Defoe clearly demonstrates the power of this positive affirmation in his acclaimed novel *Robinson Crusoe,* which is often regarded as the first English novel. The lead character Robinson Crusoe, who had left England on a sea voyage, ended up on a desolate island where he spent about thirty years of his life after a horrific shipwreck which claimed the lives of all his companions. Cast onto a deserted island, Robinson Crusoe was devastated until he began weighing the plight of his situation against the positive and found that the positives far outweighed the negatives. He chose to look on the bright side. This changed him from a pessimist to a super optimist who began to take command of his life. He managed to make a remarkable success of a bad situation which he wouldn't have achieved had he allowed negativity to dominate his life. That's exactly what you must do.

9. Let this be the basis of your internal communication - what you tell yourself - the thoughts that dominate your mind.

10. Pay attention to those silent thoughts. Always activate your constructive inner dialogue.

- Stay away from negative influences such as people with negative energy. By always doing this it becomes part of you, and this will radiate outward. You will then avoid those people that exhibit the behaviour that you deem negative and spend more time with those who reflect your affirmation list. If at anytime you find yourself trying to do anything that is not on your affirmation list just leave it there. Take corrective steps immediately.

- Talk positively to yourself. Never say things such as "I can't do it." You are only limiting your potential.

Remember nothing is insurmountable. Always believe in your power to do anything. Daniel in the Old Testament survived when he was thrown into the lions' cage because of his sincere belief. He also survived when King Nebuchadnezzar ordered his servants to throw him into a blazing fire.

Daniel's story attests to the power of the mind. At a show in Fukuoka, Japan, I couldn't believe it when I saw people walking over spikes and glasses. It was amazing to me that they could eliminate the fear and activate their mind until they got truly convinced that they would not get hurt. That's exactly what happened – neither the sharp glass nor the spikes could hurt them.

This proves that the mind works in a miraculous way. So use these miracles. Project that image. People will be attracted to you if they see that you know that you are a positive person and you stay that way. If you know that you are happy and you can project it, people will notice it. The same applies if you know that you are beautiful and you can project it. Like-minded individuals will be attracted to you like a magnet.

Think about it and all the rewards that will come with you being your ideal self. Have that idealized person in you mind - either a role model or simply the real person you aspire to be. Put yourself in the picture, the situation, see that person. Refer to chapter 1 until you have perfected your battle plan.

Often people take a long and meandering way to get there when they can take the superhighway.

Key points to remember

Your thoughts are so powerful that they can make you or destroy you. Guard against negative and destructive thoughts and promote positive thinking.
Don't place any limitation when coming to positive thinking—think big and aim high and see the things that dominate your mind become real in your life.
"We can achieve anything we can imagine."

"Self-image is what meets the world."

Chapter 4

SELF-IMAGE

How to acquire a Sophisticated Success Attitude, Phenomenal Appearance and Superb Communication Skills

Success attitude, phenomenal appearance and communication skills all start with two important things: love and respect for yourself. If we can love ourselves and make a concerted effort to look after ourselves we will be a step ahead. The result is that you will feel good about yourself and people will feel the same about you.

Thus I say to you, make an effort to improve all those aspects that you feel insecure about and watch the results. You see, when YOU feel insecure about something, it simply means that you have neglected it and remember we can always do more. There is absolutely nothing to stop you.

The most important thing about life is not so much about living. It is more about being able to enjoy it. This is a universal truth. It doesn't matter where you are and what you do, life without happiness is simply not worth living.

Happiness is the most elusive of all aspirations. Some people even make the mistake of equating money with happiness. There are so many people I know who have money but are unhappy, in fact more unhappy than some of those I know who don't have money.

You find true happiness in life when you are happy with yourself (image, personality, behaviour, thoughts that dominate your mind); you have people that you like and love in your life (lovers, family, circle of friends and associates); you have money to manage your life (buy and do the things that you want); and time (to do whatever you want when you want it.) These include doing things you like when you want to do them. Many a time you can determine your happiness by making a decision and plan to stop doing those things you hate and doing only those you are passionate about.

When I first realised that it was time to change my self-image to the ultimate best I could be, I began reading some of those motivational books. I am sure you have read a couple of them yourself. They talked about things in an abstract way which still looked too far from where I was standing. What I really wanted was a formula that would show me how to do it. Not a book that talks about something without giving me a clue about how I could effect those changes.

For example, if you want to fly a plane, you can read all the books, but until you get someone or a manual that tells you exactly how to do it, giving step -by- step instructions, you will never be able to take that plane off the ground. If you were able to do that it would be by a stroke of luck, and a lot sooner than you could imagine you would have plugged it to the ground. But armed with a formidable plan of action you can get to wherever you want to be; there is literally nothing stopping you.

In order to attract the best, you must look the best. No one wants to be involved in any meaningful relationship with someone that they think is not worthy of their standards.

Here is how:

Set high Standards
Raise your standards and put them on a par with the kinds of standards you are trying to attract.

Build self-esteem
A study I conducted between 1999 and 2003 indicated that people are more attracted to those who exude confidence, and who have a high level of self-esteem. It is simple, if you don't believe in yourself, no one will believe in you.

Speak eloquently
Ever heard people say, no I don't want to see this person, he always speaks no sense, or he is boring? Always try to be brief if you have something to say.

Talk smart. Say brilliant things only and let others fill in the gaps by saying lots of other unimportant things. That way you will be remembered as a smart person that everybody wants to associate with.

Etiquette

For someone who wants to expand far beyond the domain of an average person good etiquette is not negotiable. You need to develop good manners and nurture them so that they become part of your natural or instinctive reaction pattern.

Do things in moderation

Do not overwork yourself, do things in moderation and you will last much longer and look your best. Often people tend to overindulge in activities without realising the damage they do to their body and the time they often waste. This goes for activities such as sex and eating: set limits and have boundaries.

Behaviourists believe that a person functions through the energy they generate, and that the energy you waste on one activity will not be available for another. If you can put this in your head, then you will begin to cut out some of the useless activities in order to spare the energy and time for some useful activities congruent with your goal for the ultimate best.

Go for a professional massage

Massaging your body helps you calm down as you take a break from the hectic pace of life and the plethora of activities which are a daily reality of the contemporary world. You must take a good care of yourself if you hope to look good. If you take good care of yourself, the results will show. If you don't, the results will be self-evident.

Key point to remember

Self-image is all about the way you feel about yourself—what premium you put on yourself. A good self-image radiates outwards through whatever you do.

The more positive your self-image the more positive you become, the happier you become and the more professional you become.

And the more elegant you become because everything you do, you do according to the quality you put on yourself. When you feel good about yourself you attract good things into your life.

"And this house,
which is high, shall be
astonishment to everyone
that passeth by it."

(2 Chronicles 7: 21)

Chapter 5

PHYSICAL IMAGE

How to Nurture and Project a Success Image

To be the best you simply have to look exactly that. Look the part. You must be self-promoting and in order to achieve that, you need to put value or premium quality on yourself.

The reasons behind putting value on yourself:

1. Looking exceptionally good shows that you love yourself and you take care of yourself.

2. Other people judge you based on how you look - when you look good people will feel good around you.

3. Often people tend to shun those who neglect their appearance.

4. Your appearance tells a lot about your inner self, personality and even your aspirations.
    Here's a case in point. A grand image will give you the upper hand and confidence in any situa-

tion. As far as image is concerned the picture you see in the mirror must be worth commenting on. It must be a spectacle of some sort that can keep you captivated watching it from any angle. Go back to the picture of the ultimate person in your mind and perfect that picture. Become the living equivalent of that picture.

Let me tell you a story. One day I was at a party in London and began making some silly jokes in an effort to impress a young woman I was trying to woo. She immediately withdrew and began complaining to a friend of mine about my silly behaviour. From that time onwards I knew that I had to learn how to deal with such situations if I hoped to have any success in that area.

But perhaps the most important thing to remember here is that you must aim to be unique. Discover your strengths and supercharge them. The problem with many people is that when they learn new skills and they become better people, they automatically begin to see those who are less fortunate in those (improved) areas as inferior. You must never do that. Otherwise your attempt to improve yourself can turn out to be one sorry affair that alienates you from others.

You must remember that you will always be what you are because of other people. Without their love, support, approval and appreciation you will simply not become the best you can be. The point here is that you must work with the people, not against them by having an unnecessary over-exaggerated sense of yourself. You must aim to be unique without annoying other people around you and don't be apologetic about it.

People fall for the whole package when they fall in love.

Improving your image means starting with the simplest of all things, with the task ranging from plain simplicity to intricate complexity. For example, things such as cleaning yourself properly, washing your face, toning your skin, applying the right creams, lotions and perfumes, looking after your body, eating properly (balanced food), exercising regularly, avoiding stressful situations and knowing how to handle them, and listening to your body.

As I am writing this, I am yet to encounter a person who falls for a single aspect in a person (be it a friend or a lover). It may not seem so but the truth is people take that single aspect which entices them and inevitably make it cloud the whole picture.

If the other aspects of the package shout a complete no-no, they simply forget that you exist. This is so because as human beings we are social animals and we judge on totality. We are fully aware that it is a fallacy to make any informed decision by only looking at one side of the coin. If you hope to have people looking at you with respect and admiration, you must value yourself. You are the ultimate trophy and you need to put the highest premium on that trophy to enhance its value. Remember the value of an entity depends solely on how much effort and skill is put into it. That said you need to do something! But what exactly is it that you need to do to display the ultimate prize?

Humans are typically lazy by nature and therefore old habits are often hard to get rid of. And that is the biggest obstacle to success. That is why I have devised a simple formula which is easy to apply. It is like a walk in the park.

When I was doing research for this book, many people I talked to had read self-help books. They told me that although the books made sense they did not know how to begin applying the philosophy proposed in those books. For that reason I wrote this step-by-step practical guide.

Physique

The importance of your physical presence cannot be over stressed. People who look after their physique are generally likeable, attractive and irresistible. It is common knowledge that in order to look physically good, you must make it a habit to exercise regularly, to tone your body and get rid of that excess fat. It is a health hint and the results are considerable. When you are healthy you glow; you look your best; your skin, teeth, eyes and everything about you becomes desirable. Good things unfortunately do not come cheaply, so you must be prepared to put in time and energy. You will excitedly grow into the new look that epitomizes the ultimate you.

Here is a refresher. Let me put it simply. You can't genuinely hope to attract the best, if you do not look the best. Remember the saying that birds of a feather flock together? It is the law of attraction. If you hope to succeed in everything you do, you must project a successful image. There must be sufficient evidence to prove that you are not neglecting any aspect of the overall package. Physique is top on the list. But why should physique be such an important priority. The answer is simple. It is something that you don't have to search for. If people neglect their physique that will be the first thing others notice. First impressions last.

The result of a successful projection will always be positive as the effect ripples to all areas as you become satisfied both personally and financially. We need to be well groomed in a way that will be beneficial to the advancement of our career, or give us an edge in dealing with any other area of significance that is dear to our hearts and minds.

Voice

There is nothing as important in a human being as the voice. The way you speak is really important. It is an integral part of a human being. If you have a serious problem with your voice I advise you to get help. Visiting a voice clinic will be an important investment. I personally went to the voice clinic in

Gardens, Cape Town to get voice lessons and training.

Research shows that when you speak people first focus on how you speak. If it is monotonous, what you say will be lost because the delivery is poor. So if you are not one of the few people who are gifted in this area, seek help with your voice and general communication skills. I can tell you that your voice is your most powerful weapon.

Imagine coming into a room full of strangers. These people have heard a lot about you and are expecting to hear you speak. I tell you that the first word you speak will determine the mood and the reception. If you speak with a squeaky voice, you can expect less reception from your audience and a lot of mumblings while people complain about struggling to hear you or your irritating voice. Acquire a deep sensual voice that sends people wanting to hear more. If you manage, you will become completely irresistible. You must also have the right tone because tone also communicates your inner thoughts.

Hygiene

You can follow all the steps recommended in this book or elsewhere but if you are unhygienic, you can forget it. No one will respect an unhygienic person let alone want to associate with them. Be as hygienic as you possibly can. This is one area that is completely non-negotiable. Remember the true secret of self-improvement lies in the ripple effects that it generates, by improving one area you get closer and closer to making up the improved new package. You must scrub yourself and use the best products you can afford that are suitable for you. People do react differently to different products so take care in selecting the right ones. If you don't know ask. There are people who can assist you.

Face

Your face is literally your screen. It is an open book for everyone to read. People can virtually learn anything about you by merely looking at your face. For instance, one can determine your status, your personality, and even the amount of money you have by taking one look at your face. Problems, disappointments or failures always find their way to your face, just as good health, happiness, confidence level and success do. Therefore, as your screen, your face must be well-looked after.

Here is how:

Wash your face at least twice a day and apply a good moisturiser that is suitable for your skin type. Pimples should be prevented at all costs. If your skin gives you problems try to follow a strict regimen:

1 Hands off. Keep your hands off your face; they leave lots of bacteria which cause pimples.

2 Never scrub or scratch your face. Use your bare hands to wash your face and wipe it with a clean, white face towel.

3   Use a face wash that contains a balanced formula i.e. the one that doesn't leave your skin too dry.

4   When washing your face, wet it first with luke-warm water and then massage it. Wash gently before rinsing with clean lukewarm water. If it's hot use cold water.

5   You need to tone your skin every time after wash-ing it, using a good toner and clean cotton wool to remove all the dirt.

6   Do not get tempted to squeeze a pimple – be-sides leaving a bad mark it also spills the bacteria over your skin, which is the reason why pimples often seem to grow from the same spot over and over again.

7   Avoid eating oily food.

8. Drink enough water and eat lots of fresh fruits and vegetables.

9. Taking multivitamins on a regular basis can also help to improve your skin.

10. Never skip a meal. When your stomach gets empty it secretes certain chemicals that can find their way through the bloodstream and emerge as pimples on your face.

11. Detox your face and steam it on a regular ba-sis. You can detoxify by placing ripe avocados on your face for about an hour before washing it.

12. When steaming your face, always make sure that you do not leave it too dry afterwards.

13. And finally, avoid direct exposure to the sun.

Teeth

1. Brush your teeth regularly and floss before you go to bed. Your toothbrush must be replaced every three months.

    •   You must also make it a habit to see your dentist every six months to check your teeth and have them professionally cleaned.

2. Always carry a mint in your pocket to freshen your mouth and stay away from extremely hot drinks like coffee and extremely hot food as they can cause mouth cancer.

3. Also avoid sweets! Ever seen the teeth of those children whose irresponsible parents give them too many chocolates and sweets? I am sure you have. I have and they look horrible.

    •   So stay away from chocolates, caffeine, excessive alcohol and smoking, and promote healthy white-looking teeth.

Odour

If you are from this planet you must know by now that an unpleasant smell is a complete no-no, especially for someone who is trying to be the BEST they can be.

- Bad smell can be the result of body odour or bad breath. The former can only be dealt with by washing thoroughly every day, using good soap, and applying roll-ons under your armpits and perfumes over your body and clothes. The latter can be the result of poor oral hygiene, mouth and throat infections or high acidic levels in your stomach.

- For the mouth you need to brush your teeth in the morning when you wake up and when you go to bed at night. Where possible brush your teeth after every meal.

- You need to use mouth wash. There are many products that you can buy but the best is to ask a dentist or pharmacist who can prescribe something for your unique needs.

- Eat plenty of plain yoghurts – it diminishes the smell and prevents plaque.

- For the acid in the stomach that causes an unpleasant smell in your mouth, you must drink plenty of water and try not to skip meals because that leads the stomach to secrete excessive acid which can result in an ulcer or bad breath. If your problem is serious a doctor can prescribe tablets to normalise your acid level.

Body

Wash your body at least twice a day and make sure you wash thoroughly. You will feel relaxed.

- Use the best soap with a good smell and not cheap ones that make you smell like you have been working and sweating.

- Detox your body. When you feel good you look good.

Clothes

Believe it or not, people will mostly judge you according to the way you dress. You need not blow your hard- earned cash on a shopping spree; the key is to know what is suitable for your body type/physique. You can buy and wear all the most expensive clothes in the world, but if they are not the correct match for your body you will have simply wasted your money.

- Wear the best clothes that suit you best.

Shop for only those clothes that perfectly fit your body

Everybody is unique. As a rule of thumb you must first analyse your body and personality and carefully identify the right clothing combination for your frame.

- Best clothes accentuate the good parts (strong points) of your physique while hiding your weak points. Indeed, you will know that you have bought the right clothes when they highlight your strong points and conceal the weak ones.

• You can use the service of an image consultant or stylist, but if you would like to do it yourself you must rather do pre-testing. You could for instance wear something that you feel is suitable and then visit a public place to gauge the reactions and see if you receive any compliments. If the reaction is good then you know that you are on the right track.

• Professional service is always worth the investment. *1ˢᵗ Solutions* in Cape Town is one of the top agencies that offer advice on how to dress appropriately. The agency also offers training in business etiquette, professional appearance and presentation skills. Get one of these agencies to help you work on your wardrobe and analyse your body. This will pay in a big way.

Eyes

Your eyes need to look radiant. Take enough time to relax and rest. Sleep deprivation can make your eyes look dull and puffed.

• Get enough sleep. The ultimate best has super-white eyes that radiate excitement.

• When working on the computer try to take regular breaks and gaze into the distance now and then.

• I once had red eye with red veins indicating a stressful life and unhealthy living habits. I eradicated this by placing tea bags or slices of fresh cucumber on my eyelids for at least 30 minutes once a week. This helps to sooth strained eyes. I also avoided working on the computer for too long or walking in the blazing sun without shades.

• It is also important to have your eyes tested regularly.

Unwind the body by merely relaxing or taking power naps.

Afternoon naps work wonders to improve the way you look, the way you feel and your general state of health. A nap reduces stress and helps the body to relax and heal. So make it a habit to take a nap during the day when you are at home, or when you get back from work as most people work during the day. Try to make an afternoon nap a priority if you can, and your general outlook will improve as you take time for yourself and get in touch with your inner being.

Quit smoking, it is strongly advised.

People hoping to be the best they can be must kick all destructive habits, and smoking is one of those that must be top on the list. If you can quit smoking, quit now while you still have the chance. Smoking is acknowledged as a fatal health hazard and it still shocks me to see people not doing anything about this lethal habit.

- Smoking destroys your lungs and leads to heart disease, bad smell and tuberculosis.

- There is also evidence suggesting that smoking increases the chances of acquiring mental illness.

Therefore make a conscious effort to stop smoking. There is a range of products that helps people quit or minimise the urge to smoke.

You are what you eat

- Prioritise eating fresh fruits and vegetables, fish, nuts and grains. These are some of the food that we often neglect to eat regularly.

- **Avoid excessive intake of:**

  1 Alcohol

  2 Coffee

  3 Chocolates

  4 Fizzy drinks. Opt for pure fruit juice instead.

  5 Sugar. Brown sugar is a much healthier option than white sugar.

  6 Salt

  7 Fatty foods (junk food). Opt for low-fat products.

- **Promote sufficient intake of:**

  1 Fresh fruits and vegetables

  2 Fluids

- Drink plenty of water. Your body needs fluid. You should know by now that the recommended amount of water to take daily is 8 glasses. I drink 9—an extra one to compensate for all those years when I didn't know how important it was to drink water.

Here is how:

- Take a bottle of water with you all the time. When you ride your bicycles make sure that your squeeze bottle is there and that you stop now and then to have few sips. In that way you will enjoy your water and it will become a habit.

- If you are travelling by car most of the time, always have your bottle next to you so that you can readily take a sip. While waiting at the robot, take a few sips (if it is safe to do so).

- Carry fresh fruit with you in your car: bananas, apples or grapes are easy to carry and eat.

- When going for drinks, drink lots of water beforehand. When at a restaurant ask for a glass of water while waiting for your order. Water dilutes alcohol and limits the impact of dehydration.

- Insufficient intake of water can also cause headaches and skin problems.

- Select a gym that is conveniently situated closer to your home or work- place so that you can readily pop in without necessarily having to make a long trip. The trick is to make things easy for yourself.

I had always struggled to maintain the habit of going to the gym regularly until I found a gymnasium located along the road to my workplace.

Key point to remember

Physical image cannot be left to chance. It is what the world meets.

People will often judge you on the basis of your physical image.

The ultimate best is someone who has perfected not only a self-image but a physical image as well.

Their style is elegant. It is self-promoting. When you look good people will be attracted to you.

"I will bless thee, and make thy name great; and thou shalt be a blessing."

(Genesis 11, 2)

Chapter 6

PERSONALITY

How to Acquire a Phenomenal Personality

Personality can be defined as the sum total of a person's unique traits including cognitive (mind), behavioural (actions) and attitudinal (motivation) factors. Behavioural factors are actions that are influenced by cognitive factors, which are in turn influenced by attitudinal factors. When blended together these three make up the individual's personality.

Attitude influences action thus your actions should be congruent with your thoughts which are informed by attitudinal factors. Take for instance a student in an English class, who has an anti-English attitude. Chances are that he or she is likely not to do well in the subject. There will be no motivation for her to study. However, if he or she is interested in the language they are likely to excel because of their motivation. They will have the drive and passion to learn.

Behaviour as an aspect of personality can be learned and unlearned. It is possible to acquire any personality that you desire as long as there is sufficient motivation. You must bear in mind that for someone to learn or unlearn something there should be enough motivation to drive them to change. Behaviourist BF Skinner believed in reinforcement to encourage behaviour. You can acquire positive personality and excellent manners that will attract people to you.

Manners can either drive people away from you or attract them to you. People are generally attracted to people with good manners. Note that I said generally, because there are still some people who are attracted to certain destructive behavioural patterns.

Etiquette

Etiquette can be summed up as the sum total of your basic manners or habits pertaining to basic and common things that human beings do from time to time. Etiquette is context-bound and as such differs from one context to another, especially from one culture to the next. It is based on protocol prescribed by certain institutions, ranging from society, culture, tribes, groups or even individual families. Yet it is possible to acquire manners for doing certain things from other people or cultures. As the ultimate best you must select only those manners that are well refined and top notch to augment your profile and your iconic repertoire. Your etiquette is inevitably part of your personality and will include communication and interaction with people and the manner in which you handle yourself generally.

In order to improve your self-worth seek constant approval from your inner self first and then from outside.

But how do you know that your current etiquette is not up to scratch? I have personally seen people with unattractive personalities, who nonetheless think of themselves as having pleasing personalities. It is natural that many people cannot really see who they really are, until such time that they take stock of themselves.

You can also solicit the views of other people. Many people who want to improve their behaviour rely on peer review about what works and what doesn't. However, this kind of feedback should be treated with great circumspection as it might be misleading or misinformed.

So go ahead and ask close friends to give you their thoughts about your etiquette, but treat their feedback with great care. It might be given merely to please you. For example, when asking a person if they think it's okay for you to speak with food in your mouth, someone might say they see no problem with it even though they really think is a bad habit. They may feel that telling you the truth will hurt you or cause you to dislike them.

Beware of the effects of negative and disparaging comments meant to discourage, discredit or even to destroy you.

Sometimes feedback is given as a calculated disparaging move often informed by jealousy to destroy you. This is a typical case of people giving others wrong advice knowingly to create problems for them. Human beings are a bunch of interesting creatures. People are more likely to be affected by negative comments than by positive comments which they tend to dismiss as mere flattery. So learn to deal with the negative otherwise you will be destroyed long before your ideal self sees the sunrise.

Contact
Psychologists say when you touch a person you evoke a feeling of empathy and trust and cement the bond between you. Babies, for example, like to be touched because that makes them feel exceptional. That's why some lovers often find it difficult to take their hands off each other.

I am talking of simple gestures like patting people on their shoulders for compliments and shaking hands, or giving appropriate hugs. One must always observe a strict protocol.

1. Only give people a pat on their shoulders when you compliment them and when they are close

to you. Don't go across the room just to pat a person. It will look artificial.

2. Only shake hands with people when you haven't seen them for a while or when you use a handshake as a sign of admiration. It might be for doing or saying something good, or beating you in a game or competition.

3. Only hug people that you know and only when they are comfortable with hugging. Don't force yourself on people. (I basically don't like hugging but people still hug me which I often find bizarre.)

Touching people everywhere is not acceptable. Ever heard of sexual harassment? Yes you have, and I have just reminded you.

Smile

Research has shown that a smile has an amazing effect. It will cost you nothing just to smile and make the other person feel good. Smile broadly and make people feel good around you and make them want you to be in their company all the time. In this way enticing chemicals work wonders to attract people to you without having to lift a finger.

Handshake

When shaking hands always look people straight in the eyes with a broad smile and firm handshake. Avoid doing other things like taping fingers as you shake you hands. It might be acceptable in your own backyard or area but not so acceptable to others who are not from your culture. So stick to firm handshakes.

Show an interest in others

If you want to enthral people and catapult your popularity, you must first and foremost show an interest in them. Remember their names. Let's be honest, people like hearing their names; in fact they like hearing anything about themselves. This is so because people are by nature always interested in themselves. Their names assert who they are, so if you make them aware that you know their names, they will be extremely thrilled. In turn they will think well of you just for doing this. Make sure that you pronounce these names perfectly. This sends a message that you are really interested in them and that you recognise them as important human beings. When they realise this they will instantly be drawn to you.

I learned an old technique which I'd like to share with you: mnemonics. Memorise people's names for a while so that you can store them in your long- term memory. When you meet a person, spend some time with him or her chatting and getting to know him/ her. Then ask to be reminded of their names even if you still remember. By so doing you are rehearsing the name and transferring it to your long-term memory.

Also ask for a business card or jot down the name in a notebook or small pocket diary. Transfer it to your data base at home or work with the description of the person. In this way you will never forget the person. Have you noticed that you often have to delete names from you phone book or diary because you can't remember where you met the person and who this person really is, because you have neglected to attach a small description? Your database must include the name, description, the place where you met the person and the date. In this way you can phone a person after years and tell them when you met and they will obviously remember you because you will be able to refresh their memories. As a general rule of thumb, don't call people only when you need their favour. Call them often just to check and see how they are keeping.

Remembering people's names will work for you

a. People love to hear their names.

b. People are self-promoting. That's why you will never be friends with anybody who can't remember who you are or your name.

c. People don't like feeling unimportant. Using their names makes them think that they must be important enough for you to take the trouble to remember them.

Free spirited

Don't dwell on your problems; they will have a long -term effect on your whole being. Always nourish the mind by thinking positively and choosing to ignore the worst or a negative experience. Don't let them become part of your new you. You will feel better when you think positively and that will inevitably radiate outward.

Small steps

Take small steps to change your lifestyle, one at a time if a radical change is difficult for you. Watch out for a relapse of the programme. Many people often get excited when they acquire new information and think that they can simply apply it in one day only to get discouraged later. So the trick is to start with small steps and end with giant steps.

Reflection is the best tool to learn about yourself

The following questions will help you understand yourself better and connect with positive vibrations of power, love and riches that will come to a peak in your life.

Ask yourself the right questions

How do I respond to these situations? Offer a realistic and honest answer and suggest an alternative which you think would have been the best way to deal with the problem.

You can achieve this by thinking of a situation similar to what you experienced and recall how you dealt with it.

1. Are you always easily discouraged?

2. Are you easily influenced?

3. Do you influence others?

4. In a group, do you dominate or are you the dominated?

5. Are you a shy person?

6. Are you manipulative?

7. Are you organised?

8. Are you the fighting type?

9. Are you a cheating type?

10. Are you a rumour monger?

11. In confrontation, are you likely to slap your partner or beat them with whatever object you can get without thinking twice?

12. How do you feel after confrontation?

13. Have you ever felt that an argument was your fault, or is the other party always to blame even when you are the one who started it? Who refused to stop fighting when the other party requested to do so?

14. Are you always the one who comes back to apologise?

15. Do you hold grudges, or are you always able to start afresh?

Now, on a scale of 0-5, how would you rate yourself on the following attributes? (see chapter 6 for more about these attributes)

- Exploitative/manipulative
- Arrogant
- Selfish
- Weak
- Emotional
- Dishonest
- Immature
- Rude
- Negligent

A score of more than 20 on the above signals that you have a lot to do to change your bad habits and attributes.

Now work on the alternative you have suggested and try to execute this corrective behaviour even if it means practising consciously. Believe me attitudes elude you at the time when you need them most. Good behaviour will not simply become part of your repertoire if you do not practise it.

As soon as you have mastered the above, begin to indentify the qualities you desire.

- Decide precisely what kind of a person you want to be, also determine if you want these attitudes for the short- term or the long haul, i.e. the one you would like to spend the rest of your life with. Please be honest.

• What characteristic or personality traits do you want from this ideal?

Some of the ideal personality traits are suggested in the next chapter.

Key point to remember

Your personality is an integral part of who you are.
As behaviour it can be learned.
Make sure that you acquire a winning personality fitting for the ultimate best you want to be.

"…and I smile and dream while pursuing my way through the world." Goethe *(The Sorrows of Young Werther)*

Chapter 7

CHARACTER AND HABITS

Which Best Principles and Attributes are Important to Acquire and Why?

Did you know that the most successful people who have achieved their ultimate self are always looked upon as trendsetters? It's true. They set high standards which distinguish them from ordinary people. That is the price that comes with being a celebrity and an affectionate being adored by all around you. If you have not had any reason or enough motivation to work on your own self including your personality, now you have the chance.

The point I'm making here is that when you set standards for yourself you must set them so high that it will be almost impossible for other people to reach. Don't be afraid to set high standards because you want to distinguish yourself as the ultimate and not the average. The saying that one must aim for the moon because even when they miss they would at least land among the stars is indeed appropriate here. Be conscious of the standard you are setting and let people see that you won't compromise for anything less. Invest in what you do and you will reap the rewards. Always compete with yourself and aim to improve your own record. You earn respect and recognition for beating your own record.

Bad habits such as the inability to deal with anger must be kicked out. Remember any negative energy needs to be contained and eliminated immediately. You can't afford to have anything negative in your repertoire if you are hoping to become the best.

As a pacesetter, you should aspire to be sophisticated, affectionate and generous, a free-spirited, good-hearted person who continually promotes personal growth and is superbly outstanding. You must aim to be inventive and develop a quick-witted temperament in order to live a profound life full of meaning.

The ultimate self is inherent and the power to change merely follows already established pathways.

Shape the way you live your life and set high standards with strong ethics.

Here is a revelation:

In a survey I conducted between 1999 and 2003 to determine which attributes the respondents found the most appealing, the following emerged as the most favoured. The subjects in my study said that they were more attracted to people who featured the attributes listed below. I have ranked them in order of significance and relatedness to each other. The study clearly showed that anybody who hopes to make a meaningful and long- lasting impact must develop, nurture and cherish these specialized attributes.

Professionalism

Professionalism implies a high standard of competence. The behaviour pattern exhibited by individuals generally reflects the skills and the expertise they possess. The greatest asset that every individual should strive for in all spheres of life is to be professional at what they do.

Independence

You must strive to be independent. Independence is defined by the Webster's Third New International Dictionary as "the quality or state of being independent", but further elaborated as "not subject to control by others; not subordinate; exemption from external control or support; freedom from subjection or from the influences of others". Independent people are more likely to be seen as having direction in life, as well as being strong and secure individuals.

Success

Strive for success in all areas of your life. Successful people are normally happy and independent. Remember success is not only measured by material possessions, so strive to achieve abundance in all areas of your life.

Power

The power you generate within you automatically radiates outwards. Amazingly it is that inner power that people feel. Empowered people are generally influential, principled, respectable and dominant without being oppressive.

Business Acumen

People with business acumen are hard-working people with the right mentality, intelligence and tact needed to succeed in any given trade.

Intelligence

Intelligent implies being able to manage your situation in a proficient manner.

Responsibility

Respectable people take responsibility for their actions. In the media circles there is what they call *strict liability* of the press meaning that the media is strictly liable for anything they report. They can't plead ignorance or negligence because they should have known about the consequence of anything they report. You too must be accountable for your actions and try to exercise caution and great care. Treat each and every situation with great circumspection. Responsible people are also trustworthy.

Happiness

As a person striving to be at the pinnacle of your life, you must know that you are responsible for your own happiness. If you are like many other people who are looking for it somewhere, you will never get it. That's why you need to develop yourself so that you can radiate it.

Look deep in yourself and appreciate who you are then you will bring about happiness in other people's lives too. Remember you must be a blessing rather than a throbbing pain to the people around you, be they friends or families, if you hope to be loved and appreciated. You, too, must be prepared to love and appreciate others without expecting anything in return. When that happens you will automatically get the reciprocation and you will attract like-minded people.

Benevolence/kindness/compassion

Kindness: be kind to people whether or not they are kind to you. It is part of humanity to be compassionate and kind. Make a difference in other people's lives by showing them humanity and humility—when that happens they will feel important and loved and they will always show their gratitude to you.

Adventure

An exciting life is one of true adventure, full of exploration and a host of exciting activities. We are simple creatures and the universe is created for us to explore, appreciate and conquer. A life without any adventure is dull and self-defeating. You must be open to new possibilities and explore those simple things especially those that have meaning for you. Otherwise you may miss opportunities to grow.

Which Habits Must Be Eradicated And Why?

The subjects described in the study identified the following as some of the habits or traits that they dislike about people. These are the habits you must kick out now.

Exploitation

Exploitation means using someone selfishly for your own material benefit with no regard for the other party. Exploitation is often characterized by violence, manipulation and deceit. Exploitative people exploit others for their own self-fulfilment or enrichment, and they care only about themselves. In her book *Tina, My Story,* the rock sensation Tina Turner aptly sketches many forms of exploitation in her relationship with her then husband.

Arrogance

Typically arrogant people are disrespectful, self-centred and often make spiteful remarks. No one in their right frame of mind wants to be near that type of person. People striving to be their ultimate best will do well do eradicate this behavioural pattern.

Selfishness
Selfish people are self-centred, greedy and narrow-minded. They care only about themselves and don't think about others.

Emotion
Over emotional people usually have poor coping skills. These are people who often can't control their emotions. They are often apprehensive and are generally reliant on others for support.

Manipulation
Manipulative people ill-treat others. They are also self-centred control freaks who derive pleasure by pushing people around and often draw them into making wrong decisions or taking ill-considered actions. These actions can have negative consequences for those manipulated while benefiting the manipulator.

Distrust
Unfaithfulness characterises this quality. Untrustworthy people are deceitful, traitorous or dishonest.

Immaturity
People with this personality attribute often have an underdeveloped sense of discretion; they are childish and are unable to face tough situations.

Negligence
Negligence refers to "carelessness with regard to one's duty or business, lack of necessary ordinary

care in doing something". These kinds of people often don't care about things and people around them, including children and their significant others.

Bigotry

Research has proven that a fixed -mind personality is amongst the most disastrous of all attributes. When people have this kind of personality, they will ask you about something and when you tell them the answer they do not want to hear, they become cynical and cling to what they wanted to hear. The unfortunate part of it is that they honestly believe that they are right, despite there being no evidence. The only thing they want to hear is what conforms to the patterns fixed in their minds. If you are inclined to bigotry, you will need to change this if you hope to cross the bridge to the ultimate self.

Here is how:

- Have a bag that you can kick really hard when you are really angry. In this way you are releasing your anger from your system. You will feel better afterwards. Oftentimes people don't release their anger which ends up magnifying itself into something big that is detrimental to well-being.

- Get stress balls to relieve stress, when you feel overpowered by negative energy or emotions.

- Always put things in perspective and never disadvantage another individual.

- Avoid arguments. If you happen to be involved in disagreements with other people always listen to their side of the story and try to see things from their perspective.

- You can learn a lot about yourself if you listen. Usually when people are angry, they become irrational and only listen to what they want to hear. You must break this habit so that you can solve your problems amicably, learn from others and grow.

- Acknowledge your mistakes and correct them immediately.

- Say sorry when you hurt another person by mistake. It is the most effective way to heal your guilt and soothe the aggrieved. It works both ways.

- Don't ever hold grudges. If you do so you are imprisoning yourself by refusing to let go of the destructive energy trapped in your system. You can't move on with your life if you are still holding grudges. You must make it a habit to forgive and move on.

- Keep your word. If you promise to do something for someone, always deliver or let them know if you can't so that you don't have to feel guilty. They will respect you for your honesty and your integrity will remain intact.

- Never satisfy yourself at the expense of another person. Be considerate all the time when you deal with other people and never knowingly disadvantage them in any way. The Scriptures say you reap what you sow: if you do something wrong to another person and you don't apologise or rectify your wrongdoing, you are likely to suffer the same fate. It is the law of nature.

Key point to remember

Kick off all negative habits and maximise the positive ones that attract positive feelings in your life. Every negative tendency must be replaced with its positive equivalent.

"The only true love affair
is with yourself."

Chapter 8

AFFECTION

How to Choose a Partner or Associates and Know if They are the Right People to Scale the Ultimate Heights with You.

An old acquaintance of mine, a professor of Journalism at a university in Australia, always reminded me that no amount of success could make up for failure on the home front. That's why I have included a chapter on this issue. The person you date can ruin you or dissipate all the energies devoted to being your ideal self. So don't make a wrong choice.

The late Jimmy Mojapelo wrote in his book *The Unknown Hero*, "The period between manhood and marriage is for some men and women one sweet smooth sailing affair; while for others it is appointments and disappointments." If you look at it, this statement applies across all the sexes. Both women and men experience a fair share of appointments and disappointments. Think about it; how many people you know in you neighbourhood, home or circle of friends who have had troubles and have chosen the wrong partner.

Some go for those who are great pretenders only to turn into monsters later, or even after they have got married. This is not fiction. I personally have had a fair share of both appointments and disappointments.

And I can tell you this: to avoid frustration and disenchantment, you must first know the right qualities you want in a partner, then you can safely find that person. This means you must know what you want and you must know yourself.

It will then be easier to find what you are looking for.

The only true love affair is with yourself.

There is an idyllic being for every one of us out there. As far I am concerned the world is abounds with people with those superlative qualities you want, but the problem is how to spot them and how to attract them. One of the fundamental questions that you must always ask yourself before you go into any relationship is, am I ready to commit? If you are not ready to commit then don't get involved, it will backfire on you. You must be ready for a relationship to work and you must go in there with your soul, heart and mind. If you are one of those people who go into a relationship with a view that you just want to try it out and see what happen, it is definitely not going to be fulfilling because you have already programmed in your mind that the relationship is tentative and that is exactly what you will get. You will consequently experience all the ups and downs because it is the energy and the signals that are being sent from the brain that this is nothing serious, at least at that stage.

This is why you must know what you want so that it can be easy for you to commit yourself once you find what you have been looking for. Think about it this way, if you attract the right partner with the qualities you want, you are guaranteed to enjoy living with them. Isn't that so? Of course you will still get an angry reprimand for leaving your shoes lying around but that's nothing compared to what many people go through.

You must be prepared to play your part to make the other party happy, so that you get what you deserve. The mistake that people often make is that once they have that ideal person, they don't maintain the relationship at that level of satisfaction. As a result, what was otherwise a good match often ends up being something else. You must remember that as innocent as you might be, you are capable of bringing out the worst in the other person and vice versa.

We have seen people going on dating shows, for example *The Bachelor*. They are trying to gain the attention of someone worthy to spend their life with. This shows how serious it is for you to find the right person to scale the ultimate heights with you. A long time ago, in many cultures across Africa and some

Asian countries, parents chose a partner for you. To-day the idea of such match-making is not popular but notwithstanding it is still practised in some communities.

If you hope to get anywhere in life, it is critical that you ally yourself with people who will complement you and not distract or destroy you. This is one aspect that shouldn't be neglected. You can scale all the heights, but if this area isn't taken care of, you will get nowhere. No matter how far you have climbed the ladder you are going to fall.

You can burn yourself out 24/7 without any progress in life at all because you have someone who keeps on doing exactly the opposite. Your partner must be someone who is ready to go the long haul with you or who is at least adaptable in those areas important to you. This applies to both sexes.

If you have attracted the opposite, then you may as well forget it. Is this someone who is bigoted, pessimistic, egocentric, careless, and has an over-exaggerated sense of themselves? Is this someone who sees you as a quick licence to a comfortable life? In that case, I have three words for you, "Give it up!" The truth is, you must be uncompromising. Unfortunately good things come to those who make them happen. If you compromise or settle for less, you get exactly that.

Here is a story from my own personal files.

For six good years I was involved in a relationship that literally drained my energy and ultimately distracted me from my priorities. I was on an acceleration curve with all my dreams within reach when I started the relationship but the upward movement immediately plummeted. This continued unabated until I decided to address the problem. For this reason it is very important to take time to get to know the person and see if their attributes will measure up to your ideal self.

Never stay in a relationship for the wrong reasons. Leave as soon as you can if you need to. Remember the saying, *"time and tide waits for no man?"* There are countless better things you could be doing than trying to work on something that is simply unworkable. If you think something is not working for you, you have guessed right. If you are done with something take your word for it. Changing minds only reflects your own vulnerability and your inability to stick with your own decision. When you betray your inner voice you become your own worst enemy in disguise.

If you have kids with someone it doesn't necessarily mean that you must marry that person if you are not happy with them and they make you feel worthless either by ridiculing you, denigrating you or belittling you through negative speech and vanity. It is sad that kids always get hurt but by staying in such relationships you are only making things worse for them. If people are in an abusive relationship this often affects the children psychologically.

How many people have you met that are stuck in a relationship for the wrong reason and are in fact unhappy? That, my friend, is a wasted life. Those are the people who will go to their grave without having lived their perfect life by being the ultimate best they could be.

Make a decision and move on and never look back. Remember only losers look back. Those who look back never progress in life because they are always concerned about their misfortunes and problems. Rather make the best that you can out of your life.

What exactly to look for in a partner (Positive Attributes)

A person on the verge of becoming the ultimate best is absolutely worthy of the finest. You deserve an exceptional partner who will not only complement your own abilities, but who will also add value to your life as the two of you together move and conquer mountains all the way to the top. Interestingly, those qualities that you look for in a partner should be the qualities that you want for yourself. It is unfair to expect one to master something that you failed to master yourself. In a relationship, partners must be able to complement each other and have the same interests. Otherwise the journey to the ideal self will just exist in your mind.

The following attributes were taken from the study I conducted between 1999 and 2003. They were identified as some of the top qualities that contemporary human beings aspire to. (See Chapter 6 for a brief overview of these attributes.)

What to look out for in a partner (Negative attributes)

As a rule of thumb, you must stay away from people exhibiting the following behavioural patterns:

- Exploitation
- Arrogance
- Selfishness
- Defensiveness
- Emotionalism (negative emotions)
- Manipulation
- Dishonesty
- Immaturity
- Rudeness
- Negligence

Don't be fooled by physical beauty. Someone exhibiting any of these attributes should be avoided. Otherwise you will live to regret the consequences of your bad choice. Remember some people are best at hiding their true colours when you first meet them. But there are always tell-tale signs if you are perceptive. If you know what you are looking for, you will always manage to spot their true colours.

But beware…here is another revelation…a paradoxical situation. In the same study men wanted the following in their ideal women:

1 beautiful, cute, irresistible (80 percent)

2 clever, intelligent, independent (73 percent)

3 warm, loving and caring (57 percent) while for women in the study an ideal man generally possessed these qualities:

3 kindness, reliability and loyalty (73 percent)

4 strength (67 percent)

5 looks, irresistibility (57 percent)

6 intelligence (53 percent)

This shows that women and men look for slightly different qualities in their ideal partners.

Other qualities mentioned for both the ideal male and female characters were business-mindedness, assertiveness, compassion and wealth. The latter element was an interesting find with about nine percent of respondents saying that their ideal character has to be rich, or "well off", as most of the respondents put it. It was interesting, but not surprising, to find that material status does indeed influence the way people judge others.

So get it into your head that some people will still judge you by your material possessions. This is sometimes linked to resourcefulness.

The important thing about affection is being able to love yourself in the way that you want other people to love you. Do not look for something in another person that you don't practise. Make sure that you develop and nurture all the qualities that you are looking for in the other person if you hope for a perfect match.

Here is how:

Self-analysis: Look deep inside yourself and see if there are any situations from the past that you haven't adequately dealt with. This is important because if you are harbouring some unresolved issues, they will manifest as destructive energy such as anger, doubts, fear, resentment, guilt, criticism and antagonism. If you don't deal with these negative emotions you will just pass them on to the next person you meet.

Release: I was at a church a couple years ago. There the pastor asked us to let go of painful past experiences that we had experienced. He asked us to close our eyes and pray for all the people who had ever wronged us, and when we finished he asked us to close our eyes and take a deep breath as we meditated. Then told us to exhale as we let go of all our anguish and free ourselves from the bondages of the past. I found this exercise so empowering.

Forgiveness: Unconditionally forgive yourself if you were the one in the wrong as well as the person who wronged you so that you can begin on a clean slate without any negative feelings trapped inside you. The best way to forgive something that has happened to you is to look at it simply as an experience that you went through and one that you will always avoid. You must always thank providence that you have at least survived because there have been people whose bad experiences that claimed their lives.

Closure: Shut the door on your dark past. Think of those bad incidents as not worth re-living. When you step out of the dark past, you move into the glowing present and illuminated future.

Victory: See yourself as a victor. That is what you are because you survived and so you are a winner. In that way you will not have any feelings of deprivation. You are ready to reach the pinnacle of success.

Key point to remember

In life, nothing comes cheaply. You must take time and make sure that you do the right thing. The choice you make today is the same choice you will face tomorrow. Any mistake you make will come back to haunt you in future.

"Positive Energy Supply Equals to Efficiency, Beauty and Success"

Chapter 9

ENERGY

How to be in High Spirits and Radiate Positive Energy and Beauty all the Time

We were told at school that energy is the ability to do work. Indeed we survive on energy. It must therefore be used effectively and not wasted. Just like electricity your own power must be preserved for good use. You must find a way to replenish it so that you are always operating at your level best.

Low energy means that you are not operating at your level best. When this happens people will notice and you will exhaust them. People want to be around those with high level energy and enthusiasm, those who inspire them and propel them to action.

Importance of listening to your body
It is crucial to nurture the source of your energy so that you can always have the amount you need. You must listen to your body so that you can pick up signs of any energy breakdown in your system. If you feel something wrong with your body, attend to

the problem immediately. Don't wait until it is too late.

If you feel down, take a day off; never pressure yourself into something if you don't feel like it. Do not force your body; treat it delicately so that it is able to carry you throughout the campaign.

Yoga is an important exercise for relaxation. A prayer can also make a huge difference. It will uplift your spirit and you will feel that you aren't alone. Ever listened to Michael Jackson's song, *You are not alone?* If you have any problem you must know that you can always trust someone.

Always take time to relax and do an activity that is relaxing. Take a stroll, and walk leisurely. When I lived in Cape Town I used to look through my apartment's window admiringly at the mighty Table Mountain and the breathtaking scenery of the Victoria and Alfred Waterfront and Robben Island across the distant seas whenever I felt down, or if I had to make a very difficult decision. After that my composure returned. That way you find positive energy from nature. This indeed reinforces the thinking that the earth is replete with everything we need to succeed in whatever we do.

Travel is the best experience
You can never hope to discover new oceans if you don't leave the shore. There is an adage in my language that says men that don't travel marry their sis-

ters. Go on a holiday to unwind from the hassle and stress.

Being in touch with nature (the world and its beautiful scenery and creatures) gives you a much-needed sense of satisfaction, peace and tranquillity and rejuvenates your mind, body and soul. A human being is an integral part of nature and this is how you can best connect with the universe.

Give your home a face-lift too

Your home is your habitat. Don't leave your living space out when you focus on energy - your environment affects you. Inject some life into it and make it lively. A superhuman with a sophisticated personality and a highly developed sense of self-worth and style is energised by a calm but trendy living space that augments their spirit and sophisticated lifestyle.

Other Important Attributes You Need To Develop

Fairness

It is important that we speak to others with respect and open minds. We must accept apologies where mistakes have been made and acknowledged and we must critically look at ourselves to see if we are fair or not.

Open-mindedness and tolerance

We must understand that in a relationship we live with people and we need to tolerate other people - because if we can't we will always be fighting.

Listening

If you hope to get anywhere in life you must develop listening skills and really understand the power of listening. When you listen you learn all the time. You become empathetic and are able to get the other person's view. This allows you to reason. Often people think that they know what others are about to say and deprive themselves of the opportunity to learn. We need to make a point without being emotional. We must be able to express concern in a precise way and straight to the point and then listen to what the other person has to say. Do not interject when someone responds or explains why certain things happen the way they did. If you do, you will never learn anything from the situation other than getting frustration and negative energy.

Managing Negative Energy and Emotions

Let go of negative energy, it is a source of anger, temper, frustration and unhappiness. We need to be calm and improve our own weaknesses and capacities to work with different personalities. The Almighty often blesses people through people they don't even like!

Thinking first before speaking ensures that only important things are said. Emotive matters need to be communicated in a constructive manner. Then they get the attention they deserve. Things such as stress need to be thoroughly managed. Deal with it effectively.

Other ways of keeping your energy at an optimum level

Keep your eyes on the prize
If you want to be a real achiever, you need to be clear about what is it that you want to accomplish. That will be the prize that you must focus on. If there is anything that distinguishes the noble people from the rest it is their ability to keep their eyes on the prize and resist temptation or any other form of destruction.

Put things in perspective
You must always put yourself in a situation before you reach a decision. Otherwise you might end up in unnecessary squabbles, or having said something that undermines the person you are trying to protect.

Respect
Developing respect as a trait works in an amazing way: when you begin to speak to someone with respect despite the circumstances, you inevitably earn a lot of respect from them. Engaging with a person in a respectful manner ensures that you remain genuine about what you are saying while being dis-

respectful always leads to one being irrational, and possibly even violent and demonic.

It is in these aspects of personality that true beauty lies. This is the kind beauty that leads to true love. Everybody knows that looks are deceiving; that is why good looks that are not accompanied by a corresponding personality remain purely physical, and cannot transmute from the physical level to the emotional level.

Improve your personality

At the risk of sounding repetitive I must remind you over and over to work on your personality presence.

- Radiate confidence

- Be polite, honest and fair.

- Say when you don't like something but always be polite unless you can't really avoid it. I am not saying you must just smile when someone is stepping on your toes knowingly to provoke you. But disappoint them by dealing with the matter in a professional way. This will prevent problems without compromising yourself and bringing yourself to their level.
Remember you are not just a victim of circumstance. You have choice.

Other ways of keeping up your energy levels

Working on mistakes and getting off with your dignity unscathed. Let's face it, everyone makes mistakes. As long as you live, you will continue to make mistakes:

So what to do?

- Learn to accept your mistakes and work on them.

- Listen to people and stop being defensive where it is not applicable.

- Put yourself in someone else's situation.

- Adopt a wider worldview that is not one-dimensional so that you rise above the lows and highs of other people around you.

- Apologise and undertake to do something about the situation.

- Do not let your mistakes becomes a burden to you.

Two people with different behavioural patterns living together can bring out the worst in each other. People are social animals, just push you will see. Marriages and relationships end up in chaos and even tragedy. These are the results for people without what I call the glue factor. There is no bonding and flowing like a stream to the river. Be peaceful – conserve your energy

Be reliable and honest

If someone tells you something in confidence, make sure that you don't get excited when you hear your friends talking about a similar circumstance. Don't add what you know. Beware of a slip of the tongue which could force you to reveal a secret.

Simply watch what you say and how you say it. A quiet person is like a closed book. Once you open your mouth people will immediately get an idea of what kind of person you are. So if you don't have anything nice to say, keep it to yourself. Keeping silent in such circumstances can conserve your energy.

Silence is Golden

If you don't have anything worthwhile to say keep quiet, more especially if it is something not nice. No one will be the wiser. Many people make a mistake of thinking that speaking all the time somehow makes them important – it doesn't. You are better off keeping quiet, if you do not have a point to make, unlike saying something that will destroy you.

Take the first initiative to do things that you want

Do that little thing that you have always wanted to do or try out. I started writing songs because I wanted to sing and I wrote my own songs. The same thing happened with acting. I wrote and produced my own movie, *Coming to Cape Town; a two world city.*

Key point to remember

There is immense energy inside each and every one of us.
You need to reach deep inside you to tap that energy, only
then will you be able to radiate positive energy and dispel the
negative.
Take care of your energy; it is an important source of your
everyday life.
Don't neglect yourself by not listening to your body.
Get enough rest, and meditate.
This nourishes your body, mind and soul.

"Call unto Me, and I will answer thee, and show thee great and mighty things."

Jeremiah 33:3

Chapter 10

SPIRITUAL DISCIPLINE

Calling on the Higher Power

The Creator wants us to succeed in our lives. He loves us. That is why He created us in his image. He is pleased when you reach your full potential and become what he created you to be – the best you can be. The Bible is a living testimony of those who came before us. In the book of Proverbs (16:3) we are reminded, "Commit thy works unto the Lord, and thy thoughts shall be established." You can use God's teachings to be the best you can be.

We are spiritual beings. Many people make the mistake of neglecting the aspect of spiritual discipline and wonder why they fail in what they try to do despite all their efforts. There is power in believing in the Omnipotent – that which we cannot see, but can only experience.

I recently read *Left To Tell*, a moving book written by Immaculée Ilibagiza, one of the survivors of the 1994 Rwandan Genocide, in which she tells of how she survived the massacre and how she managed to pick up the pieces and overcome her situation after her parents and siblings had been killed. This is how she testifies:

> "I knew that my family was at peace, but that didn't ease the pain of missing them. And I couldn't shake the crippling sorrow that seized my heart whenever I envisioned how they'd been killed. Every night I prayed to be released from my private agony, from the nightmares that haunted my sleep and troubled my days. It took a while, but as always, God answered my prayers."

God wants to help you, whatever your circumstances. He made us not to suffer but to prosper and he is there day and night if we need him and trust in him. He never disappoints. Immaculée says when God showed Himself, "I felt so liberated from grief and gravity that I began to sing for joy."

In the book of Isaiah 41:10, the Lord says, "for I am thy God: I will strengthen thee; yea, I will help thee; yea, I will uphold thee with the right hand of my righteousness." Let Him into your life and allow Him to help you. He will direct your actions and remove obstacles that stand between you and your goal. God knows what we want. As you make your goals, trust in God. This faith will help you achieve your goals more easily and faster than you ever thought.

Have faith in Him and as you pray, ask in faith and you will receive. As you place your life in His hands trusting that He will help you to be the best you can be. In the Scriptures the Lord assures us in no uncertain terms that he will not fail us as long as we ask Him with faith. "Therefore I say unto you, what things so ever ye desire, when ye pray, believe that ye receive them, and ye shall have them" (Mark 11:24)

God is the undefeated and so are you when you trust in him.

You might be distraught, ill or just going through a difficult time for whatever reason. Perhaps you have had a bad year, month, week or day. You may have lost a loved one. Or you might be feeling defeated because your dream of being *the ultimate* doesn't seem within reach anymore. Look unto the Lord, He is waiting to help you. He is strong when we are weak. God will fight all your battles if you trust in him. Send him to those areas that you find difficult to penetrate. He works in miraculous ways.

As a little boy Brian didn't believe that he could really achieve anything. He felt that his life was worthless. It was difficult to convince him otherwise as he had concluded in his mind that whatever people told him they were just saying it to make him feel better, but not achievable for someone in his position. It was just theory. Then one day a friend invited him to church. At church you often find all sorts of people with all sorts of problems. There the preacher was talking about the power of faith and how it can help one excel in all areas of their lives. "Is there anyone here who has a problem that he wants the Lord to help with?" asked the man of God. Brian and scores of people raised their hands. The priest then asked them to go to the front so that they could receive a prayer. Brian hesitated but a friend nudged him on. He found himself standing in front of a huge congregation for the first time in his life. The priest began praying for them and everyone in the church prayed.

During the prayer something happened to Brian. The feeling of being in such a powerful space with a multitude of people praying so powerfully touched his heart. He told himself that it was his last chance. He resolved to embrace the superpower. He gave his heart to the Lord. From that very same moment he was more positive and happier, despite his problems.

He was surprised that his problems were still there, but he was more hopeful about his future. What he had done was that he had transferred his problems to someone else, the Omnipotent, so they were there but he could not feel them. They were lighter and that was the beginning of his road to his ultimate best.

Open your heart to the Lord

How often have you wished that you had someone you can absolutely trust with all your problems? God is without a doubt the only Being whom you can confide in without any fear or embarrassment. He won't judge you. All you need do is to turn to him.

I say to you, ground your life in spiritual discipline and your problems will become lighter if there is someone you can trust. Often when you are alone you get scared, but when there is someone present you often feel much better. By knowing that there is someone out there you begin to glow with cheerful vigour.

Job was going through excruciating pains, his body being riddled with wounds. But even then he still trusted in the Lord. He refused to give up hope in the Lord. He knew that the Lord is the mastermind of all destines.

The Scripture is clear that if you trust in the Lord He will absolve you from all your trouble. "Blessed is the man that trusteth in the Lord, whose hope the Lord is. For he shall be as a tree planted by the waters." (Jeremiah 17:7-8)

When you trust in the Lord your life flourishes. Your life becomes complete because of His spiritual grounding. As we trust in Him, connect to His power and become secure in Him. This makes us better people who exude confidence, happiness and joy. We triumph even when there are obstacles. Just like a tree planted in the water, it doesn't die. There is a hymn that I like. Its message is so powerful that it makes me feel that I am really connecting with the Divine power in an amazing way.

There is none like you;
No one else can touch my heart like you do…

If you trust in him you won't be weak anymore. Your dream will be within reach. As you read I want you to memorise the following lines.

Lord, I place all my trust in you. You are the Lord and I know with you everything is possible. As I set off to change my life I know without doubt that you will guide me to achieve my goals. Amen.

Then close your eyes and raise your hands and say the powerful prayer you have just acquired. He is a loving God. He created the world and all that we need so that we can thrive. In 1993 I was having a conversation with an old friend of mine, the late David Segatlhe, a professor of English at the Northwest University and quite spontaneously he said, "The Lord we serve is very big, bigger than a PhD. In fact he created PhDs." I laughed this off as a joke, but over the years I began to realise the essence of that simple message. It was only then that this simple affirmation became so powerful and so true that even today this still reverberates in my mind with the same intensity.

When you live with God it becomes axiomatic to praise him and affirm his power as he works miracles in your life. He will reveal himself in so many ways. When you go through trouble he is there to help you, just look up to him and your problems will look like child's play.

Here is another powerful revelation from the Scriptures. "My grace is sufficient for you, for my strength is made perfect in weakness."(2 Corinthians 12:9) As you can see here is someone who is there all the time to help you. He is offering His true divine intervention that we often so desperately need.

When I lived in Japan a while ago, a Japanese calligraphy teacher, Mr Nobuharo Kusano asked me one day, "What are your most favourite words?"

"Dedication, discipline and commitment," I replied.

He took a nice portrait and painted these calligraphic letters:

1   Discipline – *kiristu*

2   Dedication –*iyoku*

3   Commitment -*sekinin*

For me these three words are the cornerstone of my life. They have an inherent value. Whenever I go through difficulty I recall my commitment, and recommit and rededicate. God's service is free of charge but requires commitment and self- discipline. Without discipline you are likely to falter and fall on the wayside.

In closing, I want to remind you that this is a 30-day programme. It is by no means a be-all and end-all book. Apply the programme for a month and monitor your progress. You will be amazed at how much you have learned about yourself and the world, and most importantly how much you have changed. Change is a process. Do not end there.

Key point to remember:

Have faith and your dreams will come true. The mere knowledge that there is someone out there who can listen to you when there is none to do so, someone you can turn to when you are weak or facing difficulties, is a gratifying experience.

"At the pinnacle point of your own transformation there is an incentive unsurpassed by no other form of reward—self actualisation!"

(Gilbert Motsaathebe)

Chapter 11

Other Essential Lessons
You Must Learn.

As a person on a journey to the pinnacle point you deserve all the best. That's why I am giving you this last chapter as a bonus. It has been adapted from a book I wrote entitled "*Hard Times, Simple Life: The Twenty-One Most Essential Lessons You Must Learn.*"

How to cut out people you don't want to associate with.

It is as simple as this: if you allow people to do something that you don't like, you are giving them leeway to do so. They will do it over and over again at the expense of your happiness. So set the record straight from the beginning – thus deal with things when they are small. Let them get fed up with you and leave you alone, saving you future troubles.

Go with your instinct and trust them. Do not listen too much to friends. They have the potential to mislead. They will bring you down. Friends often want to tell you what they think will make you feel better especially if you are the type that relies more on them. You need to cut destructive people completely out of your life, because if you can't, you will be unhappy for a long time. But let's say it's someone at work that you must deal with daily. Try to spend as little time with that person as possible, because sooner or later the reality of the situation will strike.

Don't be afraid to stand up for yourself.
It can be a painful experience and leave a haunting memory if you don't. You will thank yourself for the courage to stand for what is right.

A few extra tips that will help you here:

1   To tell the person that you are busy will not help you out.

2   Make it clear that, "Hey, our interests are dissimilar. What you talk about it is not my cup of tea." Speak your truth.

"I don't really like that, don't feel offended!"

"I need time to myself – I am a different person please understand."

3   Straighten up at the beginning. Tell them to "stop it right there."

Where it is difficult my personal rule is to spend at the most the maximum of 15 minutes with this type of person while at the same time looking for an excuse to get away from them.

Let go of the past, enjoy the present and look forward to the future

If only people could learn to take the lessons from the past and leave them alone, the world would be a hundred times much better place. The past has come and gone and to try to bring it back can only signal disaster. To beat yourself about something you did or something bad that happened to you will be a sure signal for failure. There is much more to life than the ugly past.

Anything that doesn't benefit you positively is not worth your time.

- Get your year planner and write down only things that matter to you, only things that you want and stick to it. Each and every time you do something which forms a step towards any of the goals go and record it there.

- Create a good memory journal and make a note next to it how to take it forward.

- Don't go back, take a step forward.

I am a firm believer that if something didn't work for you first time you are better off leaving it alone. It will only end up destroying you. Take it as a golden opportunity to get what you really wanted; what was missing from the past relationship. Remember the mere split signalled that there was a problem. Leave it alone unless something dramatic warrants it.

Beware of spendthrifts, do not become one

Some people go on a shopping spree when they have problems. These are people who cannot resist the temptation to buy everything. Ironically, most of the things that they buy are things that they don't really need. People like that buy through emotion and not rationally.

Often they have personality problems and they try to gear up their low esteem through buying things that they think will make them look good without first having worked on their inner self.

Such spendthrifts are greedy people. Again, most of these people have choice. They have little respect if any for themselves and other people. They believe that by spending money and acquiring something they gain power of some sort. The main problem with them is the hidden feeling of insecurity. Life is about balance; you need to spend your hard- earned cash wisely on things that you need. If you can't do it then you have a problem that you need to address immediately.

Don't believe everything you hear, but don't be too narcissistic either.

Have a reserved judgment. Believe but don't take it too seriously until you have proven it hundred percent. Know that people are different, so trust but don't trust too much. Many people have lost their valuables and even their lives through placing too much trust in things or people that should not be trusted.

Similarly never believe that whatever you say is true or should taken as the axiomatic truth.

Get Organized

If there is anything that we need to save, it is definitely time. The good news is learning to save time does not necessarily need one to go and do a course in time management. You can save lots of time if you take care of small things.

Get rid of Clutter.

Clutter can depress you, let alone make you inefficient. Keep your space clean. Organize your desk, your room; try to put things in order. You save time by doing things immediately and fast. Your car: take out all those small plastic wrappings from pies, sandwiches and sweets, and the empty tin cans from the car and recycle them. And do not litter. You feel better when your space is organized, tidy and collected. You feel the opposite when it is not.

Put all valuables that you use on a daily basis in one place:

Things like keys—it is much better if you put them in one place. You could save yourself a lot of time, stress and money if you do that. The best way to organize your life and save yourself the time and stress that comes with it is to know where you keep things like keys. Develop a strict habit or routine and always put them there. Create a place where you can hang the keys each time you get in and never forget to do so. Think about it: you can give a very wrong impression because you can't find your keys or that important file you need, or you have misplaced you wallet or your passport. For instance, in the past I was sometimes late for very important appointments simply because I couldn't find my car keys. So I learned the basis of putting things in their proper places.

Put your clothes away - even when you have a domestic

Always put your clothes on the hanger when you take them off or into the laundry basket. I wear my suit several times before I take it to the dry cleaners, so each and every time I take it off, it will have to go on the hanger and then the wardrobe always whether I am in a hurry or not. So develop that habit and you will see your space remaining neat and uncluttered.

Do things in advance and avoid leaving them till the last minute

I paid a heavy price for doing things at the last minute. Doing things timeously makes you competent and effective. It can put you ahead of your competitors. Time is money, money goes back to time, and you could have used that time somewhere.

Never put off till tomorrow what you can do to-day – act promptly.

If you have a task that you can do now, do it and get it out of the way. It will save you a lot if time and lot of stress. It is like taking a burden off your shoulders. Do as much as you can while you l have the time. For example, if you have to do something in the morning and you find yourself with time before then rather use it to do what you need to and don't wait until the morning to do so. It will save you the hassle in the morning rush.

Keep agonies and worries at bay

Stop worrying – it is the great source of stress. Negative energy can destroy you, because people with these feelings always expect the worst – it won't disappoint you if you expect it. This is one amazing secret about the inner workings of the mind.

Forget it all together and stop worrying about that which you cannot change, concentrate only on those things that you can change – there is no need at all to start beating yourself up, it is a futile war, which only nails you the ground.

You become your own enemy and take an active part in destroying yourself – remember you must always aim to be self-promoting. Consider your life as a mountain which your sole purpose is to climb. How far can you climb? Surely you would mount far above the ground and climb as high as you potentially can - stretch yourself to the limits.

Appreciate those small and simple things.

Appreciate small and simple things, in order to enhance your life and enjoy it to the fullest. Live outside the box and never limit your own thoughts, for the thoughts are the battleground where everything about our lives is constructed, modified and perfected. Our entire life is apprehended within our thoughts. Do not look at life as that steep uphill, but rather as a simple and nourishing experience that requires you to do the best and move along the right direction, a person armed with the formula from how to be the ultimate best, can never go wrong, should be able to enjoy life and almost effortlessly bring about those changes and adjustments that they want in their lives.

Give everything you do the best shot

When you do something give it your all, otherwise don't do it. Love profusely. Otherwise don't love at all. That should be your maxim. Do everything you do to your full potential; give it your best shot.

Inspire your soul through reading

Read books that offer examples. Read inspiring stories only and close your mind to all those that imprison you. You see a series of statements without any examples will hardly be of any help. Until you apply the principles or actionable plan you can't obtain results.

Always try to be true to yourself, and develop your own unique self.

Doctrine, faith, religion and creed

If you are Christian or have some sort of underlying motivating belief apply it to get your life out of the ordinary. Nelson Mandela used his deep belief in human potential and was kept afloat by his political party, the African National Congress.

Key point to remember

Appreciate those small and simple things in life.
Always try to be true to yourself when
faced with tough situations.
Beware of spendthrifts, do not become one.
Give everything you do your best shot.
Let go of the past, enjoy the present and look
forward to the future with confidence.
Don't be afraid to stand up for your-
self, if you don't no one else will.
Never put off till tomorrow what you
can do today – act promptly.
Keep agonies and worries at bay, if you want to be happy.

Further Reading/Bibliography

Defoe, Daniel. *Robinson Crusoe*

Holy Bible – King James Version 1611. Bible Society of South Africa: Cape Town (For all the Scriptures quoted.)

Ilibagiza, Immaculée. *Left to Tell: Discovering God amidst the Rwandan Holocaust.* Johannesburg: Hay House, 2006.

Luther-King, Martin. *I have a dream speech* (For an empowering speech quoted in Chapter 2.)

Mandela, Nelson. *I am Prepared to Die.* Mandela's speech at the Rivonia trial of 1964. (For an empowering speech quoted in Chapter 2.) (http://www.cgcannualconference.ca) (Accessed on 20 January 2008)

Mojapelo, Jimmy. *The Unknown Hero.* South Africa: Ravan, 1983.

Motsaathebe, Gilbert. *The Battle of the Sexes on TV: Gendered roles, Images and Behavioural Patterns in the Soap Opera Generations.* Thesis, Northwest University, 2003. (For insights on traits and behavioural attributes used elsewhere in this book.)

Oprah Magazine. "In My Skin" *O-The Oprah Magazine*, South Africa. Vol. 3 Number 11. November 2004 p36 (For an inspiring article about Noeleen Maholwana-Sangqu quoted in Chapter 1.)